ROMAN KARTASHEVSKY

Crawling Out of Hell

A Raw Story + Real Advice to Change Your Life

2025© Roman Crown Publishing

First published by Roman Crown Publishing 2025

First edition

ISBN: 8397634118

This book was professionally typeset on Reedsy.
Find out more at reedsy.com

Contents

Preface

There was a time when I had no dreams and no direction.

No money. No education. No faith in myself.

I was trapped in a self-destructive lifestyle—drinking too much, smoking heavily, skipping school.

Every day felt like a sequel to a movie no one wanted to watch — and I was the lead actor.

I truly believed my destiny was either construction or factory work — with occasional smoke breaks and dreams of a better reincarnation.

In my mind, my future was already written: either sweating at a construction site or buried behind some factory machine. Nothing more. Nothing better.

But today...

Everything is different.

I'm writing this book to you from Europe.

I hold a master's degree in physical education from a European university.

I've been committed to sports for years now.

I don't drink. I don't smoke.

I've earned multiple qualifications, served in the military, improved my health, and even started my own online business.

In the coming years, I plan to leave behind all forms of employment I don't believe in — and fully dedicate myself to doing what I love.

Soon, I'll become a citizen of a European country.

And just recently, I became the proud father of a beautiful son.

For me, this means *everything.*

For me, this is **victory**.

And if that guy from my past is reading this — I've got one message for him: hang in there, man. It gets good.

Introduction

Well then... hello there.

I'm 35 years old and this is my first book.

Why did I decide to write it?

Simple — I believe my life has been intense, unpredictable, and maybe even inspiring enough to serve as an example.

Not just for young men — for anyone who's ever felt lost or stuck.

The purpose of this book is clear:

To **motivate**.

To help people improve their lives.

I'll take you deep inside the world I came from — a so-called "third-rate" country — and offer you real, practical advice.

Advice that helped *me* take the first steps forward.

Advice that might help *you*, too.

Now, maybe you're thinking:

"Who are you to give me advice? What have you even accomplished?"

Fair question.

And the truth is — I'm nobody special.

I'm not famous. I'm not rich. I'm not a motivational guru in a suit.

I'm just a regular guy, like you.

But maybe that's exactly *why* this story might speak to you.

Because it's real. And because I've lived through the pain, confusion, and darkness you might be going through now.

And somehow, I found a way out.

So I'm going to tell you everything — openly and honestly — even when it's not easy.

Let's begin.

If you're stuck in a spiral of problems,

If it feels like the world is against you,

If you've stopped believing in a better future —

This book is for you.

Who am I?

I was born in Chișinău, the capital of Moldova.

My parents kept moving — always searching for a better life.

My mom is Belarusian, my dad is Russian, and somewhere in our family tree is a Polish ancestor.

Today, I don't fully identify as Belarusian or Russian. I consider myself a **citizen of the world**.

And I *feel* European.

My family?

They're educated people. Everyone has a university degree.

But that didn't mean life was easy.

Despite their education, I still had to walk the hard road —

the road of an ordinary kid starting from nothing.

Now, I'll tell you how it all unfolded...

START
HERE.
"Good luck. It will hurt.

1

Chapter 1. Too Lively

From early childhood, I was a ball of energy — constantly moving, constantly pushing boundaries.

Today, in Europe or the U.S., people would probably say I had ADHD.

Back then? I was just considered *a handful.*

I couldn't sit still.

I ran, jumped, poked, prodded, and caused all kinds of mischief.

Why? I don't know.

But I was definitely a difficult child.

Let me tell you about a few pranks I still remember — and trust me, there were plenty.

Once, when I was out walking with my grandfather, I would twist his finger constantly — trying to hurt him.

He always bore it bravely. Of course, I was tiny and probably couldn't do much damage... but I tried anyway.

At the time, I lived in **Moldova**, with my grandparents. I must've been there for about two years.

I still have warm, sun-soaked memories of that place:

Golden sunlight.

Peaches and apricots on the trees.

Grapes growing everywhere.

Once, my grandmother took me to the market. That's where I saw chewing gum for the first time — **Juicy Fruit**, I think.

It was lying right there on an open counter.

So what did I do?

I tried to steal it.

Crazy, right?

I was born into an educated family... and I'm trying to snatch a piece of gum like some street punk.

But I didn't get away with it. The vendor saw me and started shouting.

My grandmother? Furious. I got punished, of course. And I deserved it.

That was my debut in the criminal underworld — Juicy Fruit gum and absolutely no escape plan.

I also remember fighting with a local Moldovan boy. We argued over something, and I punched him right in the face.

I was five years old. Five!

Another day, my grandfather was in the garage, working on his old **Moskvich**.

For some reason, I started fiddling with the door lock... and I accidentally **locked him inside**.

He didn't have the keys.

We had to call a specialist to come unlock it.

Luckily, no one got hurt — just some frayed nerves.

In that moment, I became the youngest kidnapper in Moldova's history.

Then there was the time I found a weird pair of crooked scissors at home. What did I do?

I cut a big, beautiful **living room carpet**.

Not just that — I also shredded the cover of the armchair.

Why? I have no idea.

I just... did it. Carpet? Shredded. Armchair? Destroyed. Grandma's pride? In pieces.

But the worst — and most dangerous — thing I did?

We were visiting some relatives, and outside their house was a **gas cylinder**.

Somehow, I found a piece of paper, threw it near the cylinder, and **set it on fire**.

Plan B? Didn't exist. Plan A was: 'Let's see what happens if I light something next to gas.' Genius move.

To this day, I don't understand what I was thinking.

Thankfully, the adults noticed quickly and put out the fire.

No one was hurt — by pure luck.

You can imagine what life was like for my grandparents.

At some point, they even wrote to my parents, begging them to come get me sooner.

By then, my mom, dad, and little brother were already living in

Belarus.

And yet — despite all the chaos — my grandmother never gave up on me.

When I was just 4 or 5, she was already teaching me how to **read, write, and count**.

She did everything she could to set me on the right path.

I'll never forget that.

I'm endlessly grateful to my grandparents — for their patience, their strength, and their love.

Maybe it's thanks to them that I'm sitting here today, typing this story somewhere in Europe...

2

Chapter 2. The Village. The Dreamer

Okay, hold on.

I know I promised you motivation and advice — and it's

coming.

But first, I want you to truly **know** me.

This journey begins in childhood — with the raw, uncomfortable parts.

I'll show you how I messed up my life... and then how I fixed it.

So remember one thing:

Never give up. Keep moving forward.

As Rocky Balboa once said:

"It's not about how hard you hit. It's about how hard you can get hit and keep moving forward."

After about two years in Moldova, my parents took me to **Belarus**.

They were probably hoping for a quieter, safer life.

Back then, there was a growing hostility toward Russians in Moldova — similar to the global tension today.

We moved to a small **village**, settling in an apartment.

My younger brother and I attended the local school. He was two years younger than me.

He was calm, thoughtful — my mother's favorite.

I was the opposite: wild, rebellious, impossible to manage.

Still... I was the best student in class.

But let's be honest — competition wasn't exactly fierce. Sometimes I think the neighbor's goat had a shot at second place.

There were only a few of us — typical village kids from poor families.

Their parents were **collective farmers**.

Alcohol was everywhere: cheap vodka, homemade wine, toxic surrogates.

It was part of the culture.

I'll talk more about **alcohol** later — it's a key part of this story.

Belarus is a country ruled by one man.

And drunk, broken people are easier to control.

Some of what I'm going to tell you may shock you.

But that was my reality.

Try to imagine it.

Our school was four kilometers away.

There were no buses.

We walked — every day, in every season.

Eight kilometers round trip, In every weather — rain, snow, hurricane, or just a regular Monday. Sometimes the wind almost knocked me over.

But I kept walking.

What helped me survive it all?

My **imagination**.

As a kid, I was a dreamer.

I invented stories in my head.

I imagined I had electric powers.

Or that I could control fire.

Dinosaurs, robots, battles — I lived in those fantasies.

So much so that the real world often disappeared.

I'd walk to school talking to myself.

Sometimes a kind farmer would give us a ride on his cart.

Halfway to school, there was a **farm**.

Not a neat, modern one — no.

It was full of collapsing barns and mud.

Hungry, dirty animals.

You could smell **manure from a kilometer away**.

We wore **knee-high rubber boots** just to survive the path.

One day, a friend of mine got **stuck in the manure**.

The more he struggled, the deeper he sank.

Our PE teacher, who rode a tiny bicycle, saved him.

He huffed and puffed up the hill like a locomotive.

My friend's boot stayed buried in the muck.

Near the school, there was a sweet old lady with an **apple orchard**.

Sometimes she gave us fruit.

I also remember strange green balls near the stream — weird plants we'd pop just for fun.

We played simple games.

We'd dig a hole, place a stick inside, then hit it with another stick.

Whoever sent it flying the farthest — won.

Or we'd just run around. That was fun enough.

We lived close to a forest. People said **wolves** lived there.

Sometimes, my parents and I went mushroom picking.

My dad, back then, was still a good man.

But my parents fought constantly.

From a young age, I was drawn to **bad company**.

There was a boy in the village — let's call him **Billy**.

His father was a violent alcoholic.

At six years old, Billy was already **drinking vodka and smoking cigarettes**.

I remember once, his father carried him in his arms —

Billy had drunk too much and nearly died.

Somehow, he survived.

He taught me to smoke.

My parents kept cigarettes in a cabinet to repel moths.

Billy convinced me to steal a few.

We smoked on the balcony.

But I don't blame him.

He was just copying the adults around him.

Billy and I were close.

We had another friend — let's call him **Joe**.

He lived in a grimy railroad city and only visited his grandma occasionally.

Joe had the first **gaming console** I ever saw — an 8-bit. That was the moment I started believing in miracles. Those pixels looked like the future.

We played **Battletoads**.

It was magic.

He also told **scary stories** about his hometown —

Places where you could get beaten just for being a stranger.

Alcohol. Violence. Fights. That was normal.

Even as a child, I was surrounded by **aggression**.

Billy often hung out with older kids — cruel ones.

I remember swimming in a muddy pond and getting **shot at with slingshots**.

They used twisted V-shaped wires. It was terrifying.

Sometimes, I used **acting** to survive.

If someone tried to hit me, I'd pretend it hurt badly — just to stop them.

I was peaceful.

But when I got angry, I didn't care about anything.

Our class had **lice**.

Yes, lice.

That's how poor we were.

There was no real work — just the collective farm.

Communism, poverty, and the only real joy for adults?

Alcohol.

There was one man in the village — like a dirty, drunk **Robinson Crusoe**.

Huge beard. Always shouting. Always drunk.

We stole fruit sometimes.

Once, I was sitting in an apple tree when the owner yelled, grabbed an axe, and **chased my friend**. He was riding a bike with an axe in his hand!

I hid up in the tree.

Would he have actually hurt us? I still wonder.

I was small, skinny, and always hungry.

I craved sweets so badly, I **stole money** from my parents to buy candy and lemonade.

We hid candies in the forest, under rocks — like buried treasure. Today they'd call it a survival cache. Back then — just poor kids with wild imaginations.

I didn't help my parents.

I just ran through the streets.

One game?

Sneaking up on drunk men, kicking them from behind, and running.

They'd yell and chase us — but never caught us.

It felt hilarious.

Adrenaline.

We'd argue about who hit harder:

"If I punch you, you'll fly to heaven!"

That was my world.

That was the **village life** I knew.

I lived there for about four years.

And I dreamed — always dreamed — of escaping. And I didn't mean vacation. I wanted a teleporter, a rocket — or at least a one-way bus ticket.

3

Chapter 3. The City. My Father

After a few years in the village, my parents moved us to a city — well, a "big" city by the standards of our small country. Something like **Omaha or Miami** — not the capital, but important.

It was near the Russian border, so the **language, culture, and mentality** were basically Russian. In short — you didn't need a passport to cross the border. Just swearing loud enough usually worked.

My brother and I were enrolled in a well-regarded **gymnasium** that specialized in **math and art**.

Despite coming from a tiny village school, I quickly rose to one of the top of my class — at least in **fifth grade**.

That year, I lived with my **father**.

My mother and brother stayed behind at first.

They were supposed to join us later — and eventually, they did.

But the year I spent alone with my dad...

It was one of the **hardest** of my life.

The house he bought was primitive.

No plumbing. No toilet. No heating system.

Only a **wood-burning stove**. Welcome to survival mode: DIY edition — don't freeze, don't cry.

We carried water from a public pump —

At first with buckets,

Later using a **large aluminum container strapped to a cart**, to carry more at once.

The house was **ancient** — pre-WWII, wooden, crooked.

Before us, strangers had lived there — not family.

They had made some bizarre repairs.

Whoever lived there before had a strange obsession with **nails** — they were hammered everywhere. I don't know who lived there before us, but I suspect they were trying to build an indoor bunker — one nail at a time.

The walls were layered with thick wallpaper — **one on top of another**, maybe ten times.

Inside the walls, **rats and mice** lived.

We had to chop firewood, light the stove, survive freezing winters.

No TV.

No entertainment.

Just silence and survival.

That year, I became a **reader**.

I devoured books from our home library:

Ivanhoe, *The Adventures of Tom Sawyer and Huckleberry Finn*, and many others.

I was obsessed with **knights, kings, castles, England**, great battles, honor.

Honestly?

That was probably the **year I read the most** in my life.

Books became my **escape**.

My father?

He was... complicated.

I don't want to paint him as a villain.

I just want you to understand **what shaped me**.

Sometimes, he'd explode with **rage**. There was no TV in the house, but the family drama aired live.

He'd **push me onto the couch**, shout, threaten with his fists.

He'd insult me, call me names.

He'd say things like he could "break me."

Yes, I was difficult.

But is that how a father should act?

Maybe that's why I started to **hate him**.

Later, I even turned my younger brother against him.

When my dad wasn't home, I'd **cut the wires from his computer**,

Mock him,

Steal money from him.

It's hard to admit now... but I was angry.

And I wanted revenge.
As a little kid, I saw him as the **perfect father**.
But something in him **broke**.
He began traveling for work — gone more and more often.
And worst of all?
He showed **no interest** in us.
Not in me. Not in my brother.
He was just... **absent**.

One day, when I was a teenager, he just **left**.
He moved to **Russia**, met another woman...
And we stayed with Mom.

My mother was a **language teacher** — French and German.
It was her **dream job**.
She had a degree from **Minsk University**.
A good person.
But also difficult.
She constantly nagged and criticized my father — often over small things.
And he'd snap.
They were both **hot-headed**.
Arguments were constant.
Right in front of us.
We heard everything.
It never turned physical —
We were an **educated family**, after all.
But the **emotional violence**?
The shouting?
The insults?
Those left scars.

My father never hit me.

But he could **humiliate** me with words.

And that hurt in ways that lasted for years.

Even now, I know:

Those experiences gave me **psychological trauma**.

But they also gave me clarity.

I **swore** that when I become a father,

I will **always be present**,

Always care,

Always listen.

Because that's what kids need most.

Not perfection. Just... attention.

4

Chapter 4. Gymnasium. Mistakes

Let me tell you a bit about the gymnasium I attended.

For a 'prestigious gymnasium,' we had more fights than math contests.

There were some really smart kids — actual geniuses in **math** and **art**. At that school, it was cool to be **smart**.

But it was also cool to **smoke behind the school building**.

Fights? Of course.

The classic teenage ritual: a circle of kids, shoving, shouting, laughing.

And yeah — I was part of that chaos too.

One memory still burns in my mind.

I once said something inappropriate to a teacher — just a careless comment.

Some kids decided that I had "**betrayed the group**."

On our way to the theater, one of them **shoved me from behind**.

I smashed my head against a pole.

Even now, if I met that guy and he gave me the slightest reason...

I'd probably want to hit him.

Some things are hard to forgive.

Another time, in winter, we were having a snowball fight — just kids being kids.

But someone **threw a frozen snowball** right into my face.

It **broke my nose**. I was bleeding.

I looked into his eyes...

There was **no anger, no laughter — just hatred**.

Pure, dark hatred.

That was our school.

That was the **atmosphere**.

Here's another story — it just came back to me.

I was in fifth or sixth grade. We were playing basketball.

Among us was a **Romani boy**. He constantly insulted everyone —

Saying things we didn't even understand.

He was arrogant. Untouchable.

Like a **Terminator without brakes**.

One day, I lost it.

He stepped up to me — confident, fearless.

I ran toward him and **kicked him like Bruce Lee**.

He didn't fall. So I swung my fist and **hit him in the face**.

Blood.

To my surprise...

He admitted he was wrong.

Now, let me be clear.

Violence is never the answer.

If you live in a civilized country —

Don't do what I did.

You can walk away.

Talk it out.

Ignore it.

Back then, I didn't know any better.

But I've noticed something:

Some guys become kinder after getting punched.

It's a sad truth from where I grew up.

I'm not proud of it.

But that's how it was.

Once during PE, I accidentally kicked another guy's ball.

He came at me — ready to punch.

I blocked the first strike.

But then... I **let him hit me**.

Why?

I don't know.

I could've fought back — but I didn't.

Maybe I was tired. Maybe I felt guilty.

Sometimes, **I just didn't want to fight anymore**.

Another time, I fought a **heavy guy**.

He pinned me down with his weight.

I couldn't move.

I couldn't breathe.

I lost.

And as you can see —

I lost often.

I was a **troublemaker**.

Laughing, running wild, doing stupid stuff.

And again — I made an old mistake.

I befriended the **worst guy possible**.

Let's call him **Matt**.

At first, the cool guys in class welcomed me.

But then I drifted away — probably because I started **skipping school**.

Matt was a thief.

He stole from classmates and failed in school. For him, school hallways were basically supermarkets — just without the checkout lines.

We did dumb stuff together.

One day, we **locked the janitor in the bathroom** using a mop as a barricade.

A "funny" prank, right?

Here's my first real advice to you, dear reader:

Your environment shapes you.

If you want to grow,

Surround yourself with smart, brave, goal-oriented people.

Even if you don't notice it —

You become like the people you hang out with.

If your circle is toxic, lazy, or criminal —

Get out.

Now.

Before it drags you down too far to climb back up.

Then came **Scott**.

Around sixth grade, my father introduced me to **computer games**.

He took me to a gaming club.

I saw people playing **Counter-Strike, Warcraft III** — it was like magic.

I was hooked.

I knew — this was it.

This was my world.

Back then, in our country, computer games were treated like **pure evil**.

People panicked about addiction.

Parents freaked out.

Now, that sounds crazy —

In university, I later had a whole subject on **esports**: tournaments, player salaries, sponsorships.

Gaming is now a career.

But back then?

It ruined me.

I started **skipping school** to play.

It became an **addiction**.

My grades **plummeted**.

Eventually, I got **expelled** from the gymnasium.

I drifted from school to school.

I told one principal flat out:

"I'm not going to attend."

I didn't care anymore.

I just wanted to be in the **gaming club**. The gaming club was the only place I felt 'online.' The rest of my life was stuck in offline mode.

5

Chapter 5. Computer Club. Fights.

We had our favorite computer club.

Actually, there were several across the city — new ones opening all the time.

But this one?

This one was **our world**.

We laughed there, played endlessly, and made friends.

And right outside, on a small green patch of grass... we **fought**.

Games triggered emotions.

All the PCs were lined up side by side — no headsets, no space.

If you **insulted someone**, you'd better be ready...

Because a fist might follow. It was multiplayer — with the 'real pain' DLC.

There were always **bullies** — older guys, stronger, meaner.

They picked on the weak.

And nobody stopped them.

That's just how it was.

Let me tell you some stories.

They're all tied to **my friend Scott**.

We met in that very club — and our shared passion for games made us inseparable.

We were like brothers.

We spent nearly every day together — at the club, at home.

Both of us lived in private houses, helped our parents (when forced)...

But we hated chores.

We wanted just **one thing** —

To play. And maybe eat something.

Meanwhile, my life was **falling apart**.

I got kicked out of school — again and again.

I could have graduated from a top gymnasium, gone to university, earned a degree, gotten a great job...

But no.

Gaming consumed my future.

Although...

If this had happened in today's world?
Maybe I would've become a famous **esports player**.
All I needed was **support**.
And **discipline**.

Fights were a **daily thing**.
There was one guy — a trained **boxer**.
He always hung out with a real troublemaker —
A guy who **spit on people**, provoked, humiliated,
knowing the boxer would protect him.
They seemed massive. Unstoppable.
Once, our club admin — a big dude — got tired of it.
He **knocked the bully down** and kicked him while he was down.
It was wild. Brutal.
And, honestly, a little satisfying.

I once watched **two guys fight** on that same patch of grass.
One of them was prepared — confident, focused.
He beat the other down with clean, precise strikes.
Then he turned to me, smiled, and said something casual — like nothing had happened.
And I was jealous.
I wanted that **confidence**, that **power**, that **presence**.

Where I grew up, **strength was everything**.
Speed. Aggression. Boldness.
You wanted respect?
Be strong.
But I was... different.
Small. Skinny. Couldn't pronounce the letter "R."
Kids made fun of me.

I was cheerful, talkative — but **shy**.

I'd **steal money** from my parents to buy sweets, share with friends, and of course — spend at the club.

But when I played?

I **transformed**.

In games, I was brave. Sharp. Loud. Fearless.

Even if the guy next to me was bigger and stronger —

I might **snap**, insult him, shout.

Because the game made me forget who I was.

That was me.

One day, in the **Cyberzone** club, I screamed something nasty during a match —

Not realizing a **strong guy was right behind me**.

He punched me in the lower back.

I gasped. Couldn't breathe.

I turned and yelled, "Are you crazy?!"

He just shrugged.

"Let's go one-on-one. Outside. On the grass."

I could've gone. But I suddenly remembered... I still had courage to rebuild.

I was scared.

I didn't go.

I still regret it.

I should've faced him.

Maybe I would've lost.

Maybe not.

But I should've **stood up**.

I haven't stolen anything in years.

And I never will again.
That part of me is gone.
Still, store security guards sometimes stare at me funny.
Maybe they do that to **everyone**.

Now, it's time for my **second important piece of advice**:
If you're a guy, a man, a boy — you must train.
Taking care of your body means taking care of your mind.
Even if you live in a gentler society — it still applies.
It's not about fighting.
It's about **confidence**.
Discipline.
Self-respect.
If you're being laughed at,
If you feel like a loser —
Start **training**.
Boxing, wrestling, soccer, swimming — anything.
It will change how you walk.
How you look people in the eye.
How you speak.
And how the world responds to you.
Because like it or not —
Men respect strength.
That's how it's always been.
That's how it will always be.
Let's recap.
First advice: Stay away from bad friends.
Second advice: Train. Strength = confidence.
And here's the **third** one — and it might be the most important yet:
If you love something — chase it. No matter what.
It will lead you to success.

Ever since I started training in Muay Thai, boxing, and kickboxing, I've changed.

I've often challenged myself, faced my fears head-on.

Every time before a fight, I had to defeat my fear first.

You'll read more about that later.

6

Chapter 6. Late Maturity. Russia. Thoughts about the Army

Let me be clear — I'm not here to glorify the wrong things.

If you like teasing girls, that doesn't mean you should do it.

On the contrary — **protect girls**. Always.

What I'm talking about is something else entirely.

If you **love drawing**, for example, but your parents push you toward math or science —

Talk to them.

Explain why your passion matters.

Help them understand what makes you happy.

Because when you do what you love, your happiness spreads to everyone around you.

If my parents had supported my passion for gaming —

If they had taken me abroad to tournaments —

Maybe today I'd be a **professional esports player** with titles and sponsors.

Maybe today I'd have a fan page, sponsors, and a Red Bull-branded kidney.

Of course, esports was just emerging back then.

But **abroad**, things moved faster.

Our country was always **years behind Europe**, and even further behind the U.S.

I confirmed that later — when I moved to Europe and saw **a completely different world**:

different education, different values, different future.

In my country, after finishing the **ninth grade**, students could continue for two more years and then go to university.

But I skipped most of **10th and 11th grade**.

That's something I've regretted ever since.

At 17, I went to live with my father.

He had abandoned us long ago and now lived near **Moscow**.

He never showed interest in our lives —

but whenever we visited, he welcomed us politely.

That year, I started working as a **waiter**.

It was my first real job.

Before that, I occasionally worked in youth construction brigades back in Belarus.

Let me paint the picture for you:

A **17-year-old kid**.

No car. No driver's license. No real skills.

The only thing he knows how to do?

Play video games. Résumé? Easy: 'Professional clicker.

Yeah...

I was a **late bloomer**.

I felt like I was maturing **slower than everyone else**.

But it was there, near Moscow, that I began to understand what **work** really meant.

What **money** was.

How it's earned.

And how easily it slips away.

I lived in the **kitchen** of my father's new wife's apartment.

I slept in an armchair.

Whenever no one was home, I'd **rush to the computer** and play browser games.

When my father found out, he started **locking the door** so I couldn't access it.

There was a bowl of cookies on the table.

I was skinny. Always hungry.

And I **ate all of them**.

Eventually, they **started hiding food from me**. I'd never felt like a ninja — until I started hunting for hidden cookies.

I'm not saying who was right or wrong —

I'm just telling you how it was.

In **Russia and Belarus**, once you turn **18**, you're legally required to join the **military**.

It's **mandatory**.

I know — in developed countries, people join the army voluntarily.

But not where I come from.

There, **everyone goes**.

Unless you're rich... or lucky.

Parents are terrified.

Mothers cry.

Fathers say:

"The army will turn you into a man."

Mine said the same.

And you know what?

He was right.

Sports, Military service and my wife —

Those were the **three things that changed my life**. In that order.

I liked being a waiter.

Maybe because I worked with **beautiful girls**.

At the time, I was still a **virgin**, and it **tormented me**. It was a state of being: 100% testosterone, 0% experience.

Every day, I worked while constantly aroused, full of desire.

But I endured.

Most of my coworkers were **Uzbek and Russian girls** —

gorgeous and graceful.

And I...

I wasn't bad-looking myself.

Slim, handsome. Girls noticed. They smiled. They flirted.

But I couldn't act.

Once, at a summer camp, a beautiful girl gave me her number on a piece of paper.

And what did I do?

I **threw it away**.

I felt **awkward**.

Embarrassed.

Clueless.

Later, I regretted it — badly.

The time for **military service** was drawing near.

In Russia, service lasted **one year**.

In Belarus — **a year and a half**.

Russia is massive — and where you were sent **mattered**.

The further you were deployed, the **worse the hazing**.

There's a term:

"Dedovshchina" — an old military "tradition."

It comes from when **criminals were drafted**.

Older soldiers, known as "**dedy**" (grandfathers),

would **humiliate, abuse, and break down** the younger ones.

In Belarus, the hazing was milder.

So I decided to serve **there**.

But at first, they **rejected me**.

I was too **skinny**.

Legally, if you didn't meet the weight minimum, you were **deferred for a year**.

At that time, I felt like my life was already over. I was 18 with an existential crisis.

But my father helped me **finish high school**.

In Russia, if you had money — you could buy a diploma.

And I... I decided to go to **vocational school**.

7

Chapter 7. Vocational School. Friends. Strength

At my vocational school, you could earn a basic trade — bricklayer, cook... or in my case, **welder**. Basically, I could build walls, burn cutlets — or accidentally set something on fire. I went with option three.

The group I was placed in wasn't exactly made up of scholars.

These were **real guys** — rough, street-smart, a little wild.
But honest.
I quickly became close with one of them.
We called him **Sylvester**.
He wasn't just tough — he had **a presence**.
Fast hands. Sharp eyes.
He didn't hesitate.
He had a **younger brother**, and he protected him fiercely —
like a lion.
It said a lot about who he was.

We bonded fast.
I visited his house often.
There were always people, **music, alcohol, jokes**.
We drank, laughed, passed out on the couch...
and woke up with splitting headaches
and that strange mix of **freedom and recklessness** only youth can offer.

Two songs from that time are forever burned into my memory:
Inna – "Love" and **"Hot"**.
Whenever I hear them,
I'm instantly back in that foggy, post-party morning —
hungover, but strangely **alive**.

Sylvester had been through **a heartbreak**.
His girlfriend left him, and it hit him hard.
He never talked about it, but you could **feel it** in him.
He drank more. Smiled less.
That was our environment —
pain covered in bravado. Because instead of therapy, we grabbed

another beer and laughed until it stopped being funny.

Nobody said anything,
but everyone **felt everything**.

One story still haunts me.

Our friend **Scott** had been out walking with a girl
when **three guys jumped him** —
right in front of her.
It was humiliating.
We didn't know how bad the beating was,
but we knew one thing:
We couldn't let it go.

We found one of the guys.

He lived on the top floor of a standard apartment block.
We took the elevator up.
He opened the door.
At first, we **talked to him**.
Tried to stay cool.
But **Sylvester wasn't having it**.
He calmly **took off his sunglasses**,
and without warning,
punched him hard — right in the face.
The guy stumbled.
And that was it.
We **lined up**.
Each of us gave him **one punch**.
One by one.
No more. No less.

Sounds like a ritual. In practice — more like collective stupidity with a sense of purpose.

I was **the last**.

I remember my punch perfectly.

His head slammed into the door frame.

He recoiled, and his **father rushed in** to pull him inside.

We turned —

and **ran** down the stairs.

Then one of our guys stopped suddenly and shouted:

"Wait! Why are we running? Let's go beat up his dad too!"

Thankfully, our brains came back faster than we made it down the stairs.

Thank God we didn't.

But the fact that someone even said it...

That tells you everything about our **mindset back then**:

damaged, vengeful, violent.

As a teenager, I drank **a lot**.

We lived in a **poor neighborhood** on the edge of a Belarusian city.

Alcohol was everywhere.

Drugs? Too expensive, too rare.

So people stuck to **cheap booze**.

Some even **died** from drinking toxic, homemade garbage.

It was our local nectar of the gods — except instead of visions, you got convulsions.

That's how it was.

I remember drinking on a hill one night —

our usual spot in nature.

Suddenly, a group of **army returnees** appeared.

One of them walked straight up to another guy

and **headbutted him without warning**.

It was fast. Brutal.

Raw energy, like a storm breaking loose.
And in our world?
It made **perfect sense**.

Where I grew up,
you had to be **tough**.
Sure, things could be solved with words.
But we didn't know how.
We solved problems with **fists**.
Maybe your country moved past that years ago.
But we were **still living in it**.

One day, on my way to a friend's place,
I saw **two men fighting** in the street.
One was **fat and slow**,
the other — **skinny and quick**.
The fat guy lumbered, barely moving,
while the skinny guy danced around him,
landing blows like a boxer in a movie.
Then the fat guy picked up something to fight back.
They kept going.
No one stopped them.
I just... kept walking.
Well — not completely calmly.

Here's one that still makes me laugh.
A buddy of mine once said:
"I fought a guy way bigger than me.
I punched him... punched him...
Got tired of punching —
and just ran away!"

That's it.

That's the story.

Professional humor, I guess.

By that time, I had already been training in **kickboxing** for several years.

It was my way out.

My outlet.

My revenge — against weakness.

But more on that later. Training changed everything. Well, almost — didn't give me wisdom, but at least I wasn't an easy target anymore.

8

Chapter 8. Brother. Family.

Now I want to tell you a bit about my brother. As I mentioned, he's two years younger than me.

Looking back now, I realize I should have protected him. I should have helped him. I should have been there for him. But back then... things were different.

I was the one who hurt him more than anyone else.

And this brings me to the **fourth** piece of advice:

Remember—your family are the most important people in your life!

When we were kids, my brother loved to draw. And I... I laughed at him. I told him he wouldn't amount to anything. I was like a street-level art critic — no talent, just a lot of opinions.

That was a huge mistake. Never do that. Maybe my brother had a gift. Maybe he could have become an artist. And I broke him.

I was stronger than him. And that strength gave me power to bully. If there's a special hell for nasty older brothers, I probably already have a seat with my name on it.

Cherish your brothers and sisters. Learn from my mistakes. If you're in a fight with your sibling—make peace.

Remember: outside of your family, no one truly needs you in this world.

I've learned that. And I think it's not too late.

Now I help my brother. Of course, I don't like everything about his behavior. And he doesn't like everything about me. But I understand: when our parents are gone, it will be just the two of us.

We have to stick together. Support each other. No matter what.

So remember my **fourth** advice: Value your loved ones. They are the most precious thing you have.

9

Chapter 9. Rap and Drinking.

Let me take you back to my wild youth.
Back then, we were all into **rap** —
especially **Black American rap**:
Wu-Tang Clan, **Method Man**, **2Pac** — that *old-school* fire.
That was **our vibe**.

Around that time, a new guy joined our crew.

Let's call him **Steve**.

Steve was **obsessed with foreign rap**.

And soon enough, he got us all hooked.

We even set up a **home recording studio** at my place.

Mic from a street market, beats from the internet, lyrics from a notebook. In our heads — Grammy incoming.

Steve would rap into the mic,

we wore **baggy jeans** like in music videos,

and we thought we were the **coolest guys alive**.

We rented apartments, partied nonstop, drank beer and vodka,

chased girls, celebrated birthdays.

We lived fast, we laughed loud.

Once, I hung **off a balcony** —

from a pretty high floor.

I don't even remember it.

My friends told me later.

You might forget your own birthday, but your friends will never forget you hanging off the 10th floor.

Fun? Yeah.

Dangerous? Hell yes.

One guy in our crew used to steal **Coca-Cola from kiosks**.

Steve had **all kinds of wild friends**, mostly rappers,

and the vibe was electric.

But Steve had a **dark side**.

One day, out of **jealousy**,

he stabbed a guy in the **head with a screwdriver**.

Multiple times.

Sounds like a movie?

Nope.
Just part of my life.

I never fought with Steve or Scott.
We were **too close** for that.
But those **parties**...
Sometimes I drank so much
I'd fall **asleep on the toilet**,
and someone would **carry me to another room**.
I'd just keep sleeping.
Other times, I'd be with a girl —
and some friend would just **walk into the room**.
He did that all the time.
Our world was pure **Darwinism** —
only the strongest survived.

One of my first girlfriends?
She had **another boyfriend** I didn't even know about.
He was in the hospital.
When he got out, we met.
I said:
"Let's fight."
That's how we settled things back then.
There was no fight.
He just said:
"Take her. She's yours." Romance — Eastern style.

Another time, someone **called my girlfriend cute** at a party.
I was drunk.
So I **attacked him out of jealousy**.

And that brings me to my **fifth piece of advice**:

Limit your alcohol consumption.

I'm serious.

90% of the pain and misery in so-called **Third World countries** comes from **alcohol**.

Vodka.

Cheap beer.

Moonshine.

Poison in a bottle.

It destroys families.

Kills potential.

Steals years.

In our poor neighborhood, there were places where people mostly drank, fought, and had drunken sex. This story is about one of those places.

One guy hit another with a **brick**. Sometimes, when people were drunk, someone would pull a knife...

Alcohol shuts off your brain.

Fifteen minutes — and you're no longer yourself.

You become someone else.

Worse.

That's why I **hate clubs**.

People drink, dance, and then —

a fist flies.

Then a knife.

Then someone ends up in the **morgue**.

I'm sure it's more civilized where you live.

But let me say this:

If you drink **one beer a week** — you're already addicted.

If you drink **anything stronger** — you're already a threat to others.

Think about it:
How much **time**, **money**, and **health** would you save if you quit?

I haven't drunk in years.
Or only in **extreme moderation**.
And I feel so much better.

Drugs?
I don't have much experience.
But between **vodka and marijuana**?
I'll take marijuana any day.
That's my opinion.

To finish, let me tell you a story.

I was a teenager.
I had half a bottle of vodka in my backpack
and was looking for "**adventure.**"
And I found it.

I met a man who invited me over.
There were **random people** there.
We drank.
We ate **crab sticks**.
That wasn't dinner. That was a culinary joke. But back then it tasted like sushi.
Then I **blacked out**.
One girl looked beautiful to me.
Was she?
No.
It was just the alcohol.

Vodka comes with a romance filter. Unfortunately — no undo button.
I tried to flirt.
Then I tried to **fight**.
I yelled things I don't even remember.
Then...
A **neighbor**, an older man, came over,
put his hand on my shoulder, and said:
"Kid, get out of here.
You don't need this."
He **walked me home**.
A **good man**.

All I want is for you to understand this:
Alcohol is dangerous.
It **ruins lives**.
I've lost someone close to me because of it.
I won't go into details.
It still hurts.

Now, I have this reflex —
Whenever I see a drunk person,
I feel **aggression**
I control it. But it's there.

I **hate** drunk people who stumble around, scream, and bother others.
There are **kind drunks**, sure.
I have no issue with them.
But the loud, obnoxious ones?
The ones who yell in your face, push you, spit on you?
They better stay away.

10

Chapter 10. Our Neighborhood. Harsh Reality

I know these brutal stories might be getting old for you, my friend. But hang in there — things will change soon.

Let me tell you a story from my old life —

from that **poor country** I left behind when I came to the European Union.

You already know —
poverty and anger ruled that place.
There were **beggars everywhere** —
just like in any "civilized" country.
But unlike in Europe, where they quietly sit with signs,
in my country they were **aggressive**, sometimes even violent.
They didn't ask — they demanded. I always thought they deserved a marketing course.

I remember one day, I was heading to a store.
And like always, a **drunk beggar** approached me.
Another man begging for vodka money.
I'd dealt with people like him **dozens of times**.
But that day...
something snapped.
I had so much anger inside.
Maybe it was from life.
Maybe it was because I was training hard —
kickboxing, pushing myself every day.
He asked for money.
I **headbutted** him. Yep.
He flew backward, crashed near the checkout,
knocked over a few items.
The cashier looked at me in **shock**.
I calmly paid for my groceries and turned to leave.
He got up —
probably still drunk —
and came back to me.
"Why did you hit me?" he asked.
I was surprised. That's when I realized: headbutts may knock people down, but they don't always knock sense into them.

But I didn't hit him again.
I just walked out.

I'm not telling this story to **brag**.
He was just a **drunk**, and I lost control.
But I want you to **understand**:
That's the kind of world I grew up in.
Maybe that's why I started kickboxing —
To protect myself.
To protect others.
Or maybe...
if you believe in the **law of attraction**,
I created that world myself.
We'll talk more about that later.

One night, I was walking home — **drunk and angry**.
I punched a mailbox.
A group of guys across the street saw me.
One of them shouted, "**You think you're tough?**"
He ran toward me, ready to kick.
There were too many of them.
I **ran**.
I lost one of my flip-flops while fleeing.
At home, filled with rage,
I grabbed a **knife** and went back out looking for them.
I didn't find them.
Or my flip-flop.
Thank God.

Oh, and I almost forgot to tell you about **my neighbors**.

Each one was **worse than the last**.

To the **left** of our house lived a **chronic alcoholic**.

He didn't work.

The floorboards in his home were rotting and uneven.

He had a brother, and together they held **nonstop drinking sessions**.

One day, a stranger came to visit —

they all got drunk.

The guest **beat the brother bloody**, right in front of everyone.

I still remember it clearly.

To the **right** of us lived a **female alcoholic**.

She rarely left her house.

She **hated our family** and glared at everyone.

But oddly enough —

she had a **good son** who did everything for her.

Behind us lived **an elderly couple** —

both of them drank.

Still not laughing?

But this was **Belarus**.

This was our life.

Across the street?

A man who had been to **prison**.

He worked as a **gravedigger**.

Also collected **scrap metal** from homeless people.

I never figured out if he was saving the world or planning something darker. Probably both.

He never looked up —

always cursed under his breath.

He seemed to **hate me**.
And honestly?
I hated him too.

Once, I poured **cold water** on his son.
The boy got sick.
I think the father **held a grudge** ever since.
Also, back then, I was **stealing money** from my parents.
Maybe that man didn't want his son to follow **my example**.

So yeah...
I was surrounded by **drunks and ex-cons**.
And I **hated them all**.

Across the street, another young guy ran a **car-painting business**.
Engines roaring all the time.
Visitors nonstop.
And me?
I dreamed of **silence**.

Every time I stepped outside,
I saw people I **didn't respect, didn't trust, didn't like**.
Yes — there were a few **decent neighbors**.
A young family across the road —
we didn't talk much,
but my mom had a good relationship with them.
Still...
That wasn't the point.

When you live in a world filled with **fear, aggression, and resentment**,
you want to **escape**.

You want to **start over**.

In my country **people don't smile** at each other.
They don't say "hello" when you enter a shop.
On buses and trains,
they stare at you from under their brows —
cold and suspicious.
Why?
Because they're **tired**.
Because they're **poor**.

Salaries are low.
Food is expensive.
A car? That's a luxury.
In comparison to Europe,
we're at least **ten years behind**.
We don't sort trash.
Most guys have buzz cuts.
People openly hate **gay people**.
(Yes, it's that bad.)
Maybe it's a bit more civilized in **Minsk** —
but I'm talking about the **provinces**.
The regions.
The **real Belarus**.

Now that I live in Europe,
I can compare everything —
the **quality of life**,
food prices,
interest rates,
values.

And it's shocking.

Imagine this:
The **minimum wage** in one of the *poorest* European countries
is three or four times higher than ours.
And the **price of food**?
Roughly the same.

When I worked as a **coach**, I made $150 a month.
Enough to buy hope — on discount — and a few loaves of bread.
I survived on **cheap sausage**, **milk**, **bread**.
Clothes?
From street markets.
If I wanted to buy something from an actual mall —
I had to **save for weeks**.

Later, I got a job as a **CNC machine operator**.
There, I made **$250 a month**.
And finally...
I could save **a little**.

That's how we lived.
Now you have a rough idea of the **reality I escaped from**.

11

Chapter 11. Monika. Love and Betrayal.

To survive in my world, I had to grow **animal instincts** — **aggression**, **dominance**, **raw confidence**.

Basically, I was like a stray dog with muscles and attitude.

But over time, all that tension built up inside me...

and turned into **rage**.

I started to **hate everything** around me.

That's when a girl entered my life.

Let's call her **Monika**.

We dated for about a year and a half.

She loved **drinking beer** and **dancing to music**.

She was fun. Loud. Wild.

And to me?

She was my **first serious relationship**.

Even back then, **loyalty** mattered to me.

One day, Monika called me **crying**.

She said some guys were bothering her.

I didn't hesitate.

I called my two best friends, and we went to the address she gave us.

When we got there, there was already a **crowd** gathered.

Turned out, Monika and her friend had **insulted one of the guys' mothers**.

So it wasn't exactly as she told me.

Still — things were calm...

Until some **chubby guy** stepped toward me and said:

"Let's go. One-on-one."

I agreed. No hesitation.

We stepped aside.

Then, weirdly, he started **undressing** —

until he was standing there in just his underwear.

It was like fighting a sumo wrestler... who forgot his pants.

It was ridiculous.

But I wasn't laughing.

He was **taller, heavier, and stronger**.

I started bouncing on my feet — moving around.
He lunged and tried a **straight kick**.
I blocked it with both arms.
Felt the full weight.
He rushed in.
I remember landing one clean punch —
right to his teeth —
just before he tackled me.

When I opened my eyes,
he was standing over me.
Looked like he was about to kick.
But from the ground, I **kicked him hard in the stomach**.
He backed off,
wiped the blood from his mouth, and said:
"Okay. Fight's over."

But I wasn't done.
I was still full of fire.
Then he grabbed an **empty beer bottle**,
smashed it,
and came running at me —
a jagged weapon in his hand, screaming curses.
I always dreamed of an epic duel. This wasn't it.
I backed off.
Thankfully, someone pulled him away.
It ended there.

When I returned,
my friends were casually chatting with the same group.
Like nothing had happened.

That's when I realized:
some people go their whole lives without ever fighting.
In developed countries, people solve problems **with words**.
But in our world?
The strongest was always right.

And I still believe this:
A man should be able to **protect himself and the people he loves**.
That's why sports, health, and discipline are **non-negotiable**.

But back to **Monika**...
She had this long-time **male friend** she'd always hang out with.
They drank together, joked around.
I was the **jealous** type.
And she **fed** that jealousy.
She'd **disappear**, **ignore my calls**,
stop replying to texts.

Once, it got to the point where I agreed to meet this guy one-on-one.
I came **alone**.
He brought a **friend**.
He also brought a **pellet gun** that shot **metal BBs**.
He even showed me how it could shoot through a metal sheet.
We talked.
And agreed:
"Monika isn't worth it."
But later, I realized he **lied** to me.

Still, that fight never happened.
And in the long run?
It was for the best.

After I returned from military service,
Monika started texting me again —
saying she missed me.
But I told her:
"We're done."
I didn't want **that kind of relationship** anymore.

Because I'd already seen **too much**.

One time, I went looking for her.
Her **mom**, on crutches, opened the door.
I walked in.
Entered Monika's room.
Dim lights. Music playing.
Monika and that guy —
half-naked, making out.
They hadn't done anything yet.
But it was **obvious** where it was going.

I **snapped**.
Tried to hit the guy.
Monika blocked me.
Then her mom stormed in
and **pushed me out** of the apartment.
I slammed the door behind me and walked away.

Later, the guy called — wanted to fight.
But I was **done**.
That moment taught me something.

And here comes my **seventh piece of advice**:

Don't date girls who still want to party and "have fun."
If she's into clubs, loud music, and drinking —
don't expect anything serious.
Especially if her family is broken.

Monika's dad was a **washed-up football player**,
drank himself into ruin.
If life were a football game, he'd been red-carded years ago.
Her mom was a drunk too —
now living with **another alcoholic**.
Once I walked into their home
and saw the guy — **completely naked and drunk**, passed out on the floor.
That was their normal.

That was **our world**.

Even as a kid, I saw **darkness**.
Once, I helped stop my friend's mom from **hanging herself**.
We caught her just in time.

Sometimes I wonder:
Was that really my life?
It feels like another planet now.
And what's coming next?
Even more intense:
The army. And real training.

But let me finish with two last stories about **violence and instinct**.

One time, Monika and I were walking downtown

and stumbled across a group of **rappers** heading to fight some **skinheads**.

Monika said:

"Let's watch! This'll be fun!"

I said:

"Okay."

Both groups lined up in front of a block.

The leaders exchanged a few words.

Suddenly —

bald-headed teens charged from every direction.

It was chaos.

Monika screamed:

"Run!"

I said:

"Why? We're not involved."

Stupid move.

In movies, the main guy always walks away cool and untouched. I wasn't that guy.

Someone tapped my shoulder.

I turned.

Wild eyes.

He grabbed my sweater.

Others ran toward us.

Monika ran away.

I got **punched in the back of the head**,

fell to the ground, curled up.

They kicked me.

Honestly?

It didn't even hurt that much.

Either I was numb from emotion, or their kicks were sponsored by "soft shoes inc."

Then came the final stomp:

"Take that, b****!"

Right to my lower back.

They ran off.

I got up, brushed myself off, walked away.

Monika and our friends were hiding in a doorway.

She said:

"I fell and hurt myself while running..."

Meanwhile, I'd just been **jumped by a mob** — for nothing.

Last story.

We were walking through town on a quiet night

when a **drunk guy** started following us.

He reached out his hand:

"Gimme five!"

I **hated drunk people** — always had.

To me, they meant **danger**.

He kept shouting, following.

I stopped.

"You really want a high five?"

"Yeah, I do!"

I snapped.

A few **punches and a knee** later — he was on the ground.

People nearby said:

"Leave them alone!"

We walked away.

But he got up and followed us again,

mumbling:

"Why'd you hit me?"

We turned into a courtyard, and he finally gave up.

Looking back?

That was an **emotional breakdown**.

I'm not proud of it.

But I'm not sugarcoating anything either.

That was **my world**.

Not exactly the kind of place you'd see in a travel brochure.

Sometimes, aggression was the only way to protect your space.

Or maybe...

It was just years of **rage boiling over**.

12

Chapter 12. A New Path: College and Kickboxing

After finishing vocational school, I knew one thing for sure:

I didn't want to spend my life on construction sites.

Nothing personal against concrete... but I prefer hitting bags, not carrying them.

No welding.

No assembly.

No concrete.

I had seen enough.

Our building crews were filled with **alcoholics**.

The only things they talked about were **vodka, cursing, and women**.

I thought to myself:

Maybe there's still a chance for me to get an education.

So I applied to a **technical college**,

enrolled in a **mechatronics technician program** —

repairing machines and industrial equipment.

I did okay in my classes —

though I skipped a lot of them...

to play computer games.

My GPA was powered by Counter-Strike and instant noodles.

Old habits die hard.

But then something changed.

One day, I watched a **fight online**.

It wasn't just boxing — it was raw, brutal.

Kicks, knees, punches — everything allowed.

I was hooked.

"I have to try this."

My inner fighter woke up and yelled: "Finally! Something more useful than gaming skills!"

I searched for kickboxing gyms in my city — and found one.

My coach?

A **Master of Sport of the USSR** in boxing.

That title meant he had beaten some of the best fighters in the entire Soviet Union.

He was a fantastic boxer.

Kickboxing was his passion project.

He taught us everything — **boxing fundamentals**, **kick combinations**, **movement**.

But for some reason, his passion didn't include... sending us to real fights.

But he had one big flaw:

He almost never sent us to competitions.

We trained hard,

but we lived in a **bubble**.

No real fights.

No tournaments.

In all those years of training,

I only **sparred a few times**

and competed officially **once**.

So basically — I was a black belt in shadowboxing.

That competition?

K-1 rules — one of the toughest formats.

You're allowed to clinch, knee strike, mix everything.

I was in good shape.

But I had **zero ring experience**.

My opponent?

A tournament veteran.

Fast. Precise. Brutal.

The fight was a war.

I held my own.

In the second round, I even **pushed him into the ropes**

and tried to finish with a knee.

Missed.

Later, he caught me.

Broke my nose.

Blood everywhere.

The referee wiped it away.

I kept going.

Eventually...

my coach threw in the towel.

I knew I was done.

Couldn't breathe through one nostril.

The septum was shifted.

I saw a doctor.

"You need surgery."

I spent a few weeks in the hospital.

After the operation, I could breathe again.

But my nose was different now.

Flattened. Like most fighters.

"There go my looks," I thought. Goodbye modeling career. Hello warrior nose.

I had always been one of the good-looking kids.

But it didn't stop me.

It only **fueled the fire**.

Kickboxing became my obsession.

Actually — **Muay Thai** became my world.

I discovered **Buakaw Por Pramuk** — the legendary Thai fighter.

I watched all his matches in **K-1 Japan** —

the biggest kickboxing stage in the world.

Then I found **Masato Kobayashi** — a Japanese phenom.

His hand skills were insane.
He even knocked down Buakaw once.
That taught me something:
Even the strongest kicker has a weakness.
Buakaw's was his boxing defense.

Inspired, I **hung a heavy bag in my apartment**
and started training like a man possessed.

But I had no promoter.
No sponsors.
And in **Belarus**, professional kickboxing was nearly **non-existent**.
There was no money in it.
The system only supported **amateur sports** —
and only if your goal was the **Olympics**.
Kickboxing wasn't even on the list.

I still hold some resentment toward my coach.
He never helped me build a real career.
I trained at full intensity —
believing I'd become a **champion**.
But I was just a **naive kid**
with no support.

Still, those workouts **saved my life**.
I **quit smoking**.
Quit drinking.
Stopped partying.
I used to waste my money on nonsense —
beer, apartments, chaos.
That all changed.

I started running —

really running.

Back in school, I struggled to complete **one kilometer**.

Now?

I could run **twenty** without a problem. I went from coughing after stairs… to chasing dreams at marathon speed.

I became **flexible** —

able to kick **above my head**.

I was one of the best in the gym.

Then… my coach left.

He needed money.

He moved to **Russia**.

We were left stranded.

My training partners and I looked for new coaches —

boxing, kickboxing, MMA…

But nothing felt the same.

We were missing **something essential**.

Still, I kept going.

I trained **anywhere I could**:

- In **Finland**, working 14-hour days picking strawberries.
- Back home in **Belarus**.
- In the **forests of Poland**.

Anytime.

Anywhere.

Because I had found my **path**.

It wasn't paved. It was muddy, sweaty, and full of bruises — but it was mine.

13

Chapter 13. The Army: Fights and the School of Life

My sport gave me **confidence** and **fighting skills**.
But it was the **army** that truly toughened me up — **mentally** and **physically**.
It showed me how brutal the world can really be.

It was time to serve.
I was finally at a **healthy weight**.
I dreamed of joining an **elite unit** — something like "Spetsnaz."
I didn't even know exactly what it meant.
I just liked how it sounded. Spetsnaz? Sounded like a superhero squad. I wanted in — even if I couldn't pronounce it.
But... I couldn't **pronounce the letter "R"** properly,
and I filled out my paperwork **all wrong**.
So instead of the elite,
I ended up in the **regular infantry** —
motor rifle troops.

The first six months of service I spent near **Minsk**,
at a training base.
There, I learned to **operate an infantry fighting vehicle**.
Then, they split us up and sent us to different units around the country.
My unit?
Dropped into the **middle of nowhere** —
a complete **shithole**. Population: boredom, mosquitoes, and my broken dreams.

In training, **sergeants were gods**.
They abused their power,
confiscated phones and chargers,
screamed orders just to feel important.
One day, there was a **massive fight**.
Our squad clashed with the **VDV paratroopers**
who shared the barracks.
It was chaos.
I stood there frozen —
watching a skinny infantry guy **punch a huge paratrooper** so hard,

his **hat flew off**. That moment taught me one thing: never underestimate a man with nothing to lose... especially if he's angry and weighs 60 kilos.

A senior officer broke it up quickly.

I had my **own fights**, too.

The first one happened early in training.

Back home, I used to stay up late gaming,

and sleep half the day.

But in the army?

Cold water wash-ups.

5 AM wake-up calls.

Immediate exercises.

I was exhausted, foggy, and messing everything up.

That annoyed a lot of guys.

One of them finally stepped up,

got in my face, and started yelling.

We were **nose to nose**.

Then I remembered something my coach once told me:

"Tense your core and **headbutt straight into the nose**."

So I did. Finally! A real-life situation where video games *didn't* help — but headbutts did.

He started **bleeding** and ran to the sink.

After that?

People started **respecting me**.

The second fight came later.

We argued.

And I hit him with a **front kick**.

He flew back, crashed down.

People broke us up.
End of story.

Another time, a **crazy sergeant** tried to take the food
my mom had sent me.
I didn't argue.
I just **shoved him.**
So hard he **fell to the floor**. I guess I unlocked the secret sergeant-eject button.
He never messed with me again.

But the army wasn't just about physical hardship.
The hardest part was **mental**.
Most guys were from **tiny villages** —
aggressive, **ignorant**, **closed-minded**.
I clashed with one of them too.
He came at me over some nonsense,
and I hit him in the face with my **elbow**.
One hit.
He staggered.
People separated us.

In Belarus, there's a saying:
"**Strike first.**"
And it worked.
But let me say this to my readers in Europe or the West:
Never do that where you live.
You'll be in **real legal trouble**.
I was lucky.
I didn't face consequences.

There was one more unforgettable incident — with an **officer**.
I was struggling to cover a vehicle with a tarp,
and this officer came over.
He started yelling:
"I'm gonna beat your ass!"
I said, calmly:
"Go ahead."
So he did.
He **punched me hard in the chest**.
And then I did something **unthinkable**:
I **hit him back**. Career tip: punching your superior is usually not part of promotion strategy.

Everyone was shocked.
That kind of thing?
It doesn't happen in the army.
It could've ended really, really badly.
He screamed that he'd ruin my life,
get me kicked out, destroy my record.
But the next day?
He smiled and asked how training was going.
Because in our world —
strength is the only thing people respect.

Some guys couldn't take the pressure.
Some **ran off into the woods**.
Some **cut their wrists**.
Hazing was real.
Senior soldiers bullied the younger ones.
One guy kept **stealing,**
and they beat him **every night**.

He finally **snitched**, and the bullies went to **military jail**.
There?
They barely feed you,
you stand for hours,
and memorize codes like a robot.
And when you get out?
You still owe time —
because your sentence doesn't count as service.

Despite everything,
I believe **every man should go through the army**.
It hardens you.
It teaches you how to function under **pressure**.
It prepares you for **extreme situations**.
But now that I live in **Europe**,
I understand something:
Not everyone needs this.
You don't need to be **forced into the army at 18**
to become a strong man.

Now, for one more story —
because this one was wild.
There was a guy who kept provoking me.
One day, I snapped.
I **planted my hands on two beds**, bent my knees —
and **launched a double-legged kick** straight into his chest.
He **flew back** like a rag doll.

You might think I loved fighting.
But I didn't. I was just a skinny guy with a temper and bad timing.
I just wanted **respect**.

I was **small**, **skinny**,
and couldn't pronounce the letter "R."
That stuff makes life harder than you can imagine.

After the army, I didn't care about anything.
I walked around in uniform,
chest out,
like I could take on the whole world.
We just wanted to **fight someone**,
vent all the rage we had built up.
Because in the army?
You work like a slave,
eat barely anything,
and suffer so much stress
you turn into a **beast**.

That chapter of my life ended...
but many more adventures were just beginning.

14

Chapter 14. My Wife

My wife is an incredible woman.

We met on a dating site, shortly after I returned from the army.

Let's call her *Barbara* for the sake of this book.

Barbara is calm and balanced.

She has two qualities that matter most to me: beauty and loyalty.

She's also brave and generous.

If it weren't for her, I might have never had the courage to go abroad

She was the one who came up with the idea to go to Finland and pick strawberries.

The plan was hers — I just helped make it happen.

Like I wrote earlier, my wife is one of the three people who truly shaped me in life.

She was the first to make me realize that it was time to leave my mother's side and become independent.

Barbara had been independent since childhood.

She would save the money her parents gave her for lunch and buy things she really wanted.

She had a big impact on me.

She made me more mature.

Back in our home country, we rented a small apartment and faced the tough side of everyday life.

We've been together for over ten years now.

And recently... our son was born.

Let me tell you one story that shook me to the core.

One time, Barbara and I went on a trip with her brother and his wife.

We visited a beautiful lake in the mountains.

We were standing there, admiring the view... when I suddenly had an idea.

I *had* to climb that mountain.

Not just any mountain — the highest peak in the Tatra Mountains Rysy.

I was wearing summer sandals.

I had no climbing gear.

But I was in great shape — and I believed I could do it.

So I ran.

Literally ran.

At the bottom, the path was still flat and easy.

But as I kept going, the steps grew steeper.

Soon, I had to start climbing, reaching high with each step.

I slowed down.

Then my phone rang.

It was Barbara.

She said she was following my trail.

The woman who was physically so much weaker than me...

still went after me.

Why?

Because we were a family.

I stopped.

I thought for a moment.

Then I turned around.

We met halfway.

And we climbed down together.

That one act showed me how deeply she truly loved me.

So, my friend — if you ever see something like this in your girlfriend — hold on to her with all your strength.

This is my next piece of advice:

If your partner sacrifices something for you, helps you without asking for anything in return — don't let her go.

Girls like that are rare.

There were other moments, too — moments that proved to me that I made the right choice back when I clicked on her profile on that dating site.

We still argue.

We still have different personalities.

But we're together.

And I love my wife deeply.

I'm truly grateful for everything she's done for me.

15

Chapter 15. Chase Your Dream

There's something important I didn't tell you earlier.

After graduating from college,

I made a decision that changed my life —

I went on to **university**.

I studied while working full-time.

Five long years.

No shortcuts.
And in the end?
I graduated as a **certified physical education teacher**.
That was my way of proving to myself:
I'm not stupid.
I can study.
I can **move forward**.

And now, here's my **eighth piece of advice**:
Never think you can't do something.
You can do absolutely anything —
if you **believe it** and **take action**.

Write down a **clear plan**.
Then take **small steps** toward it every single day.
Stay focused on **one goal at a time**,
and you'll get there **much faster** than chasing ten things at once.

One of my biggest mistakes?
Trying to do **everything at once**.
I wanted to be:

- A world boxing champion
- A world kickboxing champion
- A family man
- A business owner
- A millionaire

Too many things.
Too little time.
I was basically a one-man startup with no funding.

So here's my advice:
Start with **one** goal.
Reach it.
Then move on to the next.
Life is long.
You've got time.

I'm **35** now.
I've almost finished my **master's degree** at a European university.
I've quit two jobs.
Now I work at the **best one I've ever had**.
But deep down, I know —
Working for someone else is a **dead end**.
Unless your dream is to master the photocopier and coffee machine.
What really matters?
Building something of your own.

Here in Poland, I stay calm.
I avoid conflict.
Why?
Because I'm afraid of **being deported**.
If I got into a fight with a Polish person and they reported me...
I could lose everything.
That's why no one here knows I've trained in kickboxing for over **ten years**.
It's my quiet superpower. Like Clark Kent — but with shin guards.

Sometimes people talk to me rudely,
challenge me without knowing what I'm capable of.
There was only **one fight** — in a workers' hostel.
He attacked me first.

I had no choice but to defend myself.

Those hostels were a nightmare.
People brought in by agencies.
They didn't learn the language.
They drank every night,
argued,
trashed everything.
Just **angry, chaotic people**.
I couldn't wait to leave.
Now I rent an apartment.
And I'm planning to buy my own place.
Step by step —
it's getting better.

When we first moved abroad,
it was **hell**.
My wife and I were put in a **basement hostel**.
Spiders everywhere.
Broken showers.
Toilets that didn't work.
Dirty socks lying around.
If there were Olympic medals for mess, that hostel would've swept the podium.
They placed **two married couples in a room with random men**.
We didn't stay long.
We complained and got moved —
but even there, it was just a **tiny room**
with one **mini fridge for four people**.

Most of the workers did **12-hour shifts**,

then partied and drank all weekend.
But we realized something early:
Work less. Study more.
Because in a foreign country —
language is everything.

So here's my **ninth piece of advice**:
Learn the language of the country you move to.
Even at a basic level.
Just enough to go to the store, the bank, or the doctor.

Today, my focus is on **online business**
and **investing in cryptocurrency**.
For years, I dreamed of being a PE teacher and coach.
But I realized something:
That dream won't bring me **financial freedom**.
So now I'm going after that **next level**.

But for now, let's review the **key advice** that changed my life:

- **Cut off toxic people.**Surround yourself with good, smart, and kind souls.
- **Get into sports.**It'll strengthen your body, and even more — your mind.
- **Do what you love.**And **don't be afraid to say it out loud**.
- **Love and appreciate your family.**They're your true support system
- **Don't fear the unknown.**Take bold steps.Leave the comfort zone.

And finally, a thought that's been on my mind lately.
Maybe I made a mistake.

Maybe I shouldn't have let go of my dream of becoming a **world champion**.

Or maybe I just realized that being able to walk upright at 60 is a dream too.

Maybe it's **too late**.

But maybe...

I can still achieve **something else**.

I still train.

No more sparring.

No more hits to the head.

I've taken too many already.

My memory's not the same.

That scares me. I once forgot my own birthday. True story. Cake helped me remember.

I've had stitches in my head.

A nearly split lip.

My nose? Crooked forever.

I always fought guys **bigger and stronger** than me.

But I've **never been knocked out**.

My reflexes and defense were **sharp**.

My mind was focused.

And now, dear reader, I'll leave you with this:

Despite the mistakes,

the pain,

the setbacks...

Don't be afraid to dream — and chase that dream.

Because with enough persistence...

dreams do come true.

Write down Your dreams and goals below.

16

Chapter 16. Warsaw — My First Love in Europe

Now, my friend, let me tell you about the beginning of something beautiful —

my new life in one of Europe's great cities.

A place that changed everything for me.

I'm talking about **Poland**, and its shining capital — **Warsaw**.

I absolutely love Warsaw.
To me, it feels like a **mini New York City**.
I haven't been to NYC (yet),
but from what I've seen in movies,
Warsaw gives off a similar vibe —
just with **fewer skyscrapers**.
Still, it's alive. Vibrant.
Full of people from all over the world.
On any given street, you'll hear:

- Polish
- English
- Russian
- Ukrainian
- Chinese
- And more...

It's **diverse**.
It's **open**.
It's **fresh**.

I love seeing **stylish people**, well-dressed, fit, and full of energy. Meanwhile, I used to dress like a confused PE teacher on laundry day.
And yes — I love admiring **beautiful women** on the streets of Warsaw.
People here **dress however they want**.
They're not afraid to express themselves —
even if it's bold or unusual.

And the **city itself**?

Incredible.

Skyscrapers.

Neon lights.

Modern buildings.

At night, Warsaw becomes **pure magic**.

Coming from a **poor town in a poor country**,

I was amazed by things that now seem ordinary:

Even regular **cars** blew my mind.

I used to take pictures of them. Somewhere out there, there's a folder on my old phone titled "Fancy Cars I Can't Afford (Yet)."

Now? I see **luxury vehicles** even in the small towns near Warsaw, and I don't even blink.

Warsaw has **everything**:

- A fast subway
- Buses
- Trams
- Bike lanes
- Electric scooters
- E-bikes

Each **district** has its own vibe, its own story.

There are **green parks everywhere** —

especially the legendary **Łazienki Royal Park**.

And there's one more thing I've always loved:

shoes.

Sneakers. Trainers. Sportswear.

I remember the first time I walked into a sneaker store in Warsaw.

The walls were **covered** in models I'd only seen **online**.

And I'll be honest —

I felt awkward just **walking inside**. Like a tourist at a sneaker museum. With no guide.

Now?

That awkwardness is long gone.

I could talk about Warsaw for hours.

But my goal here isn't just to praise a city.

It's to show you how powerful it can be

when you decide to **start over** in a new place.

It's not easy.

But if your heart says it's time for a **new life** —

listen.

Leaving your old world behind might be the **best decision you ever make**.

So many things about Poland impressed me.

But one of them hit me harder than anything else:

Color.

Bright colors.

On buildings.

In parks.

On clothes.

It made me feel **alive**.

Back home, everything was **gray and lifeless**.

A leftover from the **Soviet mindset**.

Here?

Even in small towns — there's **color**, **care**, **beauty**.

Outside my apartment, there are **pine trees**.

And sometimes?

Squirrels jump right past our windows. Back home, the only thing that jumped past windows was poverty.

I'm not kidding.

It's that peaceful.

I've visited other Polish cities too.

They're all:

- Clean
- Comfortable
- Thoughtfully designed

With bridges, benches, flowerbeds, and shops **within walking distance**.

And the roads?

Smooth.

Back home, riding a bike meant dodging **craters** in the street. It was less "ride" and more "extreme obstacle course."

Here?

Pure joy.

You've got **bike lanes** everywhere.

Electric scooters parked neatly on sidewalks.

It's like living in the future.

People are different too.

More polite.

More respectful.

More civilized.

They follow traffic laws.

They let you go first.

They smile at you.

They say "thank you" and "excuse me." I almost asked one guy if he was okay — I wasn't used to that kind of politeness.

And when the weekend comes?

There's always a concert, a street performer, an art exhibition.

In every way, Warsaw felt like **another planet** compared to where I came from.

A better planet.

So if you're reading this and wondering if you should move,

change cities, countries, or even continents...

I say:

If your soul craves change — go.

17

Chapter 17. The Polish People and My Jobs in Poland

Now I want to tell you about some incredible people — the **Polish**.

About their **hospitality**, **kindness**, and **willingness to help**

others.

There was a time when I worked in Poland **"na czarno"** —
which means **illegally**, without a proper contract.
Why?
Because I had quit a previous job and couldn't find a better one fast enough.
But **rent had to be paid**, so I took whatever I could find.

Most of the time, it was small side gigs.
One time, a girl hired me to **stand in line all night**
so she could register her car in the morning.

Another job?
Construction.
Simple tasks — like stripping bark off wooden boards.
But at least I worked **alone**.
No yelling.
No chaos.
Just me and the boards. We had deep conversations. Mostly one-sided.

I also helped **set up kids' events**.
A group of Polish businessmen organized parties with tents, lights, toys —
everything.
They needed someone to **unload, build, pack**.
I worked fast, gave it my all.
It was part-time — mornings and evenings.
After a few months, they called me again.
I helped more.
They even offered me a **permanent position**.

Then there was the **super packer** job — just 2–3 days.

I moved old hospital records,

stacked them on pallets,

wrapped them in plastic.

I was quick and precise.

The guys started calling me "**the super packer**." I didn't get a cape, but I packed like one of the Avengers.

It was funny... but also rewarding.

I was **good at physical labor** —

but I knew I didn't want to do it forever.

So here's my next piece of advice:

Whatever job you do — do it as well as you possibly can.

People notice.

They trust you.

They give you more responsibility.

And that gives you an edge.

Of course, not every job was a good fit.

One time, someone offered me work cleaning a **disgusting basement**.

Mopping, scrubbing.

That was **my line**.

I said no. I'll do a lot to survive — but becoming the Lord of Moldy Basements wasn't on my vision board.

Now let me tell you about a **Polish businessman** I worked for.

Let's call him **Brian**.

He was in his 40s or 50s,

had a big house inherited from his parents,

a beautiful young wife,

and teenage twin sons.

He owned **two companies**.

He sold school supplies — backpacks, notebooks, calendars — all bright, new, high-quality stuff.

It started small: **I mowed his lawn**.

I did it well, of course.

He noticed.

And then?

He offered me a **job**.

He had a warehouse next to a chicken farm.

I helped him pack, organize, and ship products.

He sold both **small packages** and **full pallets**.

Later, he moved to a bigger warehouse, and I helped him **move everything and stayed on**.

I did it all:

- Sweeping floors
- Packing orders
- Processing shipments
- Even working on a laptop
- Even driving a forklift

But it was too much for one person.

I started making mistakes — spreadsheets, prices, invoices.

After a few of them, I said to Brian:

"If I mess up again, I'll quit." Spoiler: I messed up again. My spreadsheet karma caught up with me.

And I did.

One more invoice mistake... and I left.

So what's so special about Polish people?

Let me tell you:

Brian **drove a Lexus**.

He had money.

But every day, he brought me **a hot cup of coffee** — from his own kitchen.

Why?

I was just an immigrant.

But he treated me with **respect**.

I'll never forget that.

He even **drove me home after work**.

Not bad for a guy who packed crayons for a living.

Brian, like many Poles, lived by a simple truth:

Treat others the way you want to be treated.

It always comes back to you — like a boomerang.

Let me tell you about another job.

I worked with **two Polish stonemasons**.

Strong guys. One looked like a bodybuilder.

They ran their own company: got orders, measured, laid tiles.

I helped them lift, carry, haul debris.

They paid well.

Sometimes we rode in the car, laughed, talked.

Then... back to work.

But I didn't like **how they talked**.

Jokes about women.

Crude questions.

No boundaries.
One of them even asked:
"What position did you do it with your wife last night?"
I ignored it.
They'd even **pee on the street** in front of clients.

But you know what?
One of their clients and I had a deep conversation —
about **philosophy**.
That moment made the day better.

They needed a **full-time helper**.
But I was just looking for **extra work**.
So it didn't work out.
And to be honest, their attitude wasn't for me.

What did I learn?
That **work is about more than money**.
It's about **respect**,
boundaries,
mutual decency.

18

Chapter 18. The Athlete

In this chapter, I'll repeat some things I mentioned earlier, but it's necessary to give you a full picture of the situation.

Now let's talk about something that shaped my life in ways no school ever could:

Sport.

As you know by now, it's one of the **three greatest teachers** in my journey.

At first, I fell in love — completely —
with **Muay Thai**.
Known as the **Art of Eight Limbs**,
it lets you fight with punches, kicks, elbows, and knees.
I trained in **Muay Thai**, **kickboxing**, and traditional **boxing**.
When I moved to Poland,
I joined a kickboxing gym and **continued the journey**.

Back in Belarus, I always looked up to **athletes**.
To me, being an athlete was the ultimate dream —
cool, respected, powerful.
A life of purpose and strength.
But inside?
I saw myself as just a poor kid
with low self-esteem
and zero self-worth.

Still, I loved doing **pull-ups**, **push-ups**.
I couldn't pass a pull-up bar without stopping.
But at the same time?
I smoked.
I drank.
I didn't believe I'd ever be good enough to call myself an "athlete" — even an amateur one.

My first coach — let's call him **Rocky** —
was a **Soviet boxing champion**.

A Master of Sport on the international level.
When his fighting career ended,
he turned to coaching — and his second love was Muay Thai.
So he trained us in both:
Soviet-style boxing mixed with **Thai knees and elbows**.

I trained **hard**.
But there was one problem:
he rarely let us fight.
Only a few sparring sessions with other clubs.
Only one official tournament — which I already told you about.

Inside our gym, I was **one of the best**:

- Hungry
- Skinny
- Fast
- Focused
- Mean when I had to be

But later I learned:
Without real **ring time**,
none of that really matters.

In the ring, you need more than just muscles.
You need **mental toughness**.
You need **mindset**.
And I was missing that.

Let me tell you about a few sparring sessions.
Once, we sparred with a guy from our own club.

He was "the good boxer" — but I felt levels above him.
Why?
Speed.
Timing.
Counterpunching.
I had a clean counter
— that shot where they miss and you land flush.
I nailed him with it a few times.
His blood vessels popped in his eyes.
I felt sorry for him.
I clearly won that one.

Next up?
A guy from another club.
My coach said he could do **100 muscle-ups**
and was a former gymnast.
But he was smaller than me.
Didn't scare me.

He got mad during the fight.
Started throwing wild shots.
I stayed calm.
Landed clean punches.
By the second or third round,
he was almost done.
I could have **finished him**.
But I didn't.

Even today, I think about that.
I held back.
I had **too much compassion**.

Maybe I'm a pacifist,
training for war,
but always hoping for peace.

That was pretty much the end of my "serious" fighting in Belarus.
We kept sparring.
I kept training.
But no more official fights.

Then I moved to Poland.
New country.
New gym.
New energy.

Kickboxing is similar to Muay Thai,
but with some key differences.
And this time?
My coach **took us to tournaments**.
And eventually — he took **me**.

I started training **late** in life.
I never really believed I'd be a **world champion**.
But I dreamed about it.
I entered a few tournaments.
And thought:
"If I could just win **one** medal in Poland..."
But soon,
I had **more than one**. I have a several medals now.

And that's when I knew:
I could finally call myself an **amateur athlete**.

Not because of a title.

Not because of trophies.

But because I had:

- Earned respect
- Taken hits
- Given them back
- And kept coming

Write down what You can be proud of.

19

Chapter 19. University. Master's Degree. Believing in Yourself

After spending five years studying part-time and graduating from university in my home country, I made a decision:

I didn't want to be "just another immigrant" stuck in low-paying, low-skill jobs forever.

So when I moved to Poland, I chose a new path —
a **bold**, **scary**, **beautiful** path.
I applied to the **Academy of Physical Education** in **Warsaw**.

In my group, I was the **only foreigner**.
All the other students were Polish —
polite, well-spoken, respectful.
No fights.
No macho posturing.
No chaos.
That's Europe for you.

Our courses weren't just about sports.
We studied:

- **Anatomy**
- **Philosophy**
- **English**
- **Statistics**
- **Biomechanics**
- And many other sciences

On top of that — physical activities:
football, basketball, swimming, gymnastics...
Even a hiking trip to the **Polish mountains**.
It was a full education — of both body and mind.

During those years, I met a great friend.
Let's call him **Scott**.
He was a long-distance runner —
a lean, focused guy who raced in middle- and long-distance events.

We often ran together.
Endurance is everything in my sport,
and I **enjoy** running.
Funny, right?
I used to **hate** running in school.
I could barely survive one kilometer without feeling sick.
But now —
I run freely.

Scott and I have been friends for years.
We still meet.
We still talk.
And now?
We're both **PE teachers**,
and we both coach in our own clubs.

While studying at the university, I kept training hard.
I competed in kickboxing tournaments.
Sometimes I placed third.
Sometimes second.
Sometimes first.
And finally —
we all graduated with **Master's degrees**.
That moment?
Unforgettable.

Let me tell you a story from my **first year**.
It was **philosophy class**.
Our professor — a PhD — gave us a simple assignment:
"Prepare a speech. Present it in front of the class."
Sounds easy, right?

But for me?
It was a nightmare.

You see,
I started learning **Polish** only after moving to Poland.
I passed the **B1 state exam** just to apply to the academy.
But the **real university level**?
That was a different world.
Professors spoke fast.
Used academic terms.
My classmates used slang I didn't understand.
It was like learning to swim by being thrown into the ocean.

Still, I prepared the speech.
I stood up.
Everyone stared at me.
My heart pounded.
I wanted the ground to swallow me.
I started speaking — slowly, carefully.
No one interrupted.
No one laughed.
They **listened**.

I thought to myself:
"Do they even understand what I'm saying?"
But I kept going.
And when I finished...
the professor gave me the **highest grade possible**.

I was shocked.
"No," I told him.

"Please give me a lower grade — one I actually deserve."

He looked at me and said:

"Please don't beat yourself up."

Those words hit deep.

I just nodded and sat down.

I realized that my self-esteem had been low for many years...

And since that day...

I've tried to live by them.

So, here's my next piece of advice for you, my friend:

Believe in yourself.

Accept praise for your hard work.

Don't doubt your worth.

You've come a long way.

You're allowed to stand tall.

20

Chapter 20. Working at School in Warsaw

As I mentioned earlier, in Poland I worked different kinds of jobs:

- Packing boxes in factories
- Moving pallets in warehouses

- Random physical gigs
- And eventually...

Becoming a **PE teacher** at a **private school**.
This chapter is about that last job —
and how it changed my life.

After I graduated from the **Academy of Physical Education** in Warsaw,
I was still doing whatever I could to get by.
Factory work.
Packer.
Warehouse helper.
Temporary jobs.
Then one day — **fate knocked on my door**.

One of my old university classmates posted on social media:
he was quitting his job as a PE teacher at a private school in Warsaw.
And that meant **a spot opened up**.
I didn't hesitate.
I went to the interview.
And they hired me —
just until the end of the school year.
I signed the contract.

That moment meant **everything** to me.
Finally, I was working **in my field**.
No more back-breaking labor.
No more people who didn't respect me.

Now?
I'm still at that same school.

Year two — this time, on a **three-year contract**.
And honestly?
I'm happy.
Really happy.

It's a **Catholic school** —
and the atmosphere is something else.
The kids are:

- Polite
- Kind
- Respectful
- Supportive of one another

No swearing.
No fights.
No bullying after school.
They treat the weakest students with dignity.
They **stand up for justice**.
Even in the youngest classes —
you can feel something rare:
Democracy.
Empathy.
Human decency.

And the salary?
It surprised me — in the best way.
I expected peanuts.
They paid me **much more** than I thought I'd earn as a new teacher.

And then... the gym.

Wow.
Huge.
Modern.
Beautiful.
Windows open with a **button**.
Basketball hoops **lower automatically**.
There are **tons of balls** —
all sizes, all sports.
In my childhood?
We had **one ball** — per sport.
That's it.
Here?
For basketball alone — size **5**, **6**, and **7**.
And several of each.

My coworkers?
Just like most Polish people I've met:
Kind.
Warm.
Helpful.
Welcoming.
They don't compete — they **support**.

So for now?
I've decided to stay.
At least until I can grow my own business
and finally become fully **self-employed**.
That's been my dream for a long time.

Why?
Because I hate when people try to control me.

Tell me how to live.
Order me around.
Maybe that's **trauma from the army** —
where I learned that not every superior deserves respect.

And the students?
They're **fantastic**.
Athletic.
Motivated.
Disciplined.
They know the rules.
They play fair.
They love sports.
You can't even compare them to the kids I taught in Vitebsk.

There was only one thing I struggled with at first:
Daily prayer.
Church.
Mass.
I'm not Catholic.
Technically, I'm Orthodox —
though barely.
I never prayed much.
Never really went to church.

But over time?
I got used to it.
I even learned the prayers.
And I realized something:
Maybe faith — even if not mine —
can still give people something beautiful.

Write one prayer below and say it from time to time.

21

Chapter 21. Amazon KDP

Now let me tell you about the moment my entire mindset changed.

This was when I began to understand the power of **online business** — and how it could completely transform my life.

Back in the day, like most people,
I dreamed of finding a "**good job**" —
something prestigious, stable, with a nice salary.
In my old world,
jobs like **janitor**, **plumber**, or **construction worker**
weren't respected.
But now?
I think **very differently**.
Every job matters.
Every honest income deserves respect.
There's nothing wrong with working hard
— if it puts food on the table.

Still, I didn't want to spend the rest of my life
moving boxes or laying tiles.
And then — everything changed.

After moving to Poland,
I discovered a **Polish YouTuber**
who made money online
by publishing simple notebooks on **Amazon KDP**.

I was hooked.
I watched **dozens** of his videos.
I even bought his course —
not just about publishing, but about **crypto** too.
And to this day?
I still believe this business model is genius.

You create the interior.
You design the cover.

You upload the files.
That's it.
The book doesn't even exist —
until someone buys it.
Then?
Amazon prints it.
Ships it.
Handles everything.
And you?
You earn **royalties** — from anywhere in the world.
Sounds perfect, right?

Well... not so fast.

In reality, the **competition is brutal**.
Especially in the U.S. market.
If you just publish what you **like** —
you'll get nowhere.
You have to publish what people are **searching for**.
It's not about creativity.
It's about strategy.

Then there's **marketing**.
Ads cost money.
I started running campaigns —
but I was spending **more than I earned**.
It was discouraging.
It was frustrating.

And the worst part?
Amazon can ban your account —

without warning.
Without explanation.
They suspended me **twice**.
I had to wait **months** to get my account restored.
To this day, I don't know who reviews those books
or what triggered the flags.
But I never broke any real rules.

Right now?
My account is active again.
Some of my older books are still selling.
And this very book —
the one you're reading now —
I plan to publish on **Amazon KDP** and offer worldwide.
Who knows?
Maybe it'll become a **bestseller**.
(Just leave me a nice review, okay?)

Find and write down a few online business ideas below - and try them out.

22

Chapter 22. Cryptocurrency

Now, my friend, let's talk about **another passion** of mine — something that's **completely changed the way I see money and the future**.

I'm talking about **cryptocurrency**.

I've been investing in crypto for over **two years** now.
And no — I didn't get rich overnight.
But I did change my thinking.
These days, I:

- Keep up with global politics
- Study the financial markets
- Follow macro trends
- Watch crypto content almost daily

It all started, once again,
with that **Polish blogger** I mentioned earlier.
His course was aimed at **beginners** — and I completed the whole thing.
It focused mostly on **Bitcoin** —
what it is, how it works, and why it matters.

But soon, my curiosity grew.
I started digging deeper.
Ethereum.
Altcoins.
Layer 2s.
DeFi.
On-chain data.
Airdrops.
Memecoins (yeah, even those).
I found some incredible people online —
real experts who **don't just talk — they teach**.
I watched their videos,
took notes,
and began **practicing** on my own.

Then one day, something big happened.

I received a sum of money —

and for me, at that time, it was **a lot**.

Instead of wasting it on junk,

I made a bold decision:

I **bought Bitcoin**.

And then?

The price started going **up**.

Suddenly, I had **50% more** than I started with.

I sold.

And that was it.

The moment I realized:

You really can make money in crypto.

That's when I went deeper.

I started reading.

Analyzing.

Trying different strategies.

One book in particular **changed everything** for me:

"The Bitcoin Standard" by Saifedean Ammous

That book showed me that Bitcoin isn't just some digital coin.

It's **sound money**.

A store of value.

A hedge against inflation.

A modern-day form of digital gold.

But of course — Bitcoin isn't the only one.

There are **thousands of cryptocurrencies**.

Some are solid projects.

Some are scams.

Some are jokes that made people rich overnight.

That's why I won't turn this chapter into a technical guide.

Instead?

Let me tell you the **core truth**:

!In crypto, two things matter more than anything:

- **Security**
- **Mindset**

If you ignore those —

you'll lose your money.

Guaranteed.

Now let me speak directly to **you**, my reader:

If you haven't started investing yet — **start now**.

Not recklessly.

Not all at once.

But **start**.

Why?

Because this is more than just money.

It's about building **freedom**.

It's about learning how to **save** and how to **grow** what you have.

Try this:

Set aside **10%** of your income every month.

It could go into:

- Bitcoin
- Stocks
- Index funds

- A rainy-day account
- Or even just a book that teaches you how to invest smarter

Want some reading material to start with?

These 3 books are absolute gold:

- **The Bitcoin Standard**
- **The Psychology of Money** – by Morgan Housel
- **The Richest Man in Babylon** – a timeless classic

Read them.

You'll never look at money the same way again.

I'm not a financial advisor.

But I **am** someone who grew up poor,

learned from his mistakes,

and figured out that **the system isn't built for us**.

So we have to build our own.

Here's your challenge:

Open a notebook.

Write down your income.

Write down your expenses.

Start tracking.

Start saving.

Start learning.

You don't need to get rich overnight.

You just need to start moving in the right direction.

And one day?

You'll look back
and be amazed at how far you've come.

23

Bonus Chapter 1. Nutrition and the Golden Middle

Alright, my friend —

Let me take a break from the heavy life stories and talk to you about something just as important:

Food. Fuel. Health.

A few years ago, my wife dove deep into the world of **nutrition**.
She reads articles, watches documentaries, studies ingredients.
Me?
I know **proper eating** is one of the keys to a **healthy and happy life** —
but I don't give it nearly as much attention as she does.

Sure, I try to eat **fruits**, **vegetables**, drink **milk**, eat **cottage cheese**, **porridge**,
and I even **cook soups**.
But along with all that?
I also eat **tons of junk** —
especially **sweets**.

I know how bad sugar is.
And still... I eat it.
A lot of it.

Maybe it doesn't affect me the way it affects most people.
After all, I've been **training hard for years** —
or at least... I used to.
Lately, not so much.

Recently, I watched an interview with a **Polish nutritionist**.
He said something that really stuck with me:
"In nutrition, there is no black and white."
There's no single **universal diet** that fits everyone.
No one-size-fits-all plan.
Each person has to experiment.
Each person must find their own balance.

He recommended keeping a **food diary**:

- Write down what you eat
- How you feel afterward
- What your mood is like
- What your energy is like

After a few weeks or months,
you'll start seeing patterns.
You'll know what **fuels you** — and what **drains you**.

I'll give you an example from my own life.
When I'm **training**,
I can eat almost anything —
even a mountain of sweets —
and I feel fine. Energetic. Light. Sharp.
But when I'm **not training**?
One waffle.
One cookie.
Boom.
Bloat. Sluggishness. Brain fog.

That's why I'm sharing this with you, young friend.
So you start **paying attention** to yourself.
These days, you can even use **AI apps** to track your diet
and get custom feedback.
This isn't sci-fi —
This is **2025**.

But above all —
Eat in moderation.
Back at university, we studied **Aristotle's "Golden Mean."**
And he was right.

Not too much sugar — and not none.
Not too much water — and not too little.
Not too strict — and not too wild.
The key to life is **balance**.

Eat **fruits**, **vegetables**, **whole grains**, **bread**,
some **meat**, some **fish** — all in **reasonable amounts**.
Especially fish and seafood —
they're packed with nutrients and great for your brain.
Many experts say the **Mediterranean diet** is the best in the world.
Have I tried it?
Not yet.
But maybe you should.

Watch what you eat.
Read. Learn. Experiment. Reflect.
It matters more than you think.
Proper nutrition affects your **body**,
but also your **mood**, your **energy**,
even your **thoughts**.

But don't get obsessed.
Don't fall into the trap of perfectionism.
Just stick to the **golden middle**.

Listen to your body.
Don't blindly copy influencers or trends.
Your body is unique.

Learn how it works — and it'll reward you for it.

24

Bonus Chapter 2. Why I Hate Hostels

Do you even know what a hostel is?

I'm not talking about some cozy guesthouse or a budget hotel with fresh towels and breakfast included.

No.

A **hostel** is often the cheapest, most chaotic place to sleep —

packed with strangers, noise, smells, and zero privacy.

The cheapest ones?

Dirty.

Cramped.

Sometimes crawling with cockroaches, spiders, or even rats.

And the people?

Often drunk, aggressive, or just straight-up broken.

Of course, there are **exceptions**.

I once stayed at a nice hostel when I was taking my official Polish language exam —

but it cost a lot more than average.

And now...

Let me tell you about two hostels I'll never forget.

St. Petersburg, Russia

My wife and I were returning from Finland.

We had just finished a strawberry-picking job and were heading back to Belarus.

To save money, we booked a cheap hostel in St. Petersburg.

Men and women were separated.

I greeted the guys in my room, made my bed, shook hands — and then left to explore the city with my wife.

When I came back that night...

My bed was flipped over.

Only mine.

Food scraps, trash, and pasta were scattered all over the floor.

And the guys?

Pretending like nothing happened.

It was a **power play**.

Flip the new guy's bed.

Show dominance.

What they didn’t know?

I wasn’t that kind of guy.

I asked calmly:

— “Who did this?”

The biggest one shrugged:

— “No idea.”

He was lying there, scrolling on his phone like a king.

I asked again.

Still no answers.

Then he raised his voice:

— “Don’t piss me off.”

That’s when I lost it.

I stepped in.

Launched a quick combo straight to his face.

He tried to block — too late.

Another guy jumped off the bed and rushed me.

I threw him by instinct —

he smashed into the bed frame and split his eyebrow wide open.

Blood hit the floor.

The third guy woke up and ran straight out the door.

A guy from the front desk came in, shouting.

My wife came too.

They pulled me aside.

But I wasn’t done.

I went outside, grabbed a wooden board —

ready to finish the job.

It didn’t come to that.

They apologized.

The hostel promised to evict them.

Turns out they were **friends of the owner**.

Living there for free.

Doing whatever they wanted.

Until that night.

After that, they were kicked out.

I got moved to a different room.

But later that night, lying in bed, I heard voices through the wall:

— "Tomorrow we'll get him. Jump him in the morning. Beat the crap out of him."

I didn't sleep at all.

In the morning, I told my wife:

— "Wait here. I'll go out first."

But weirdly?

No one was there.

They never showed up.

A Migrant workers' hostel in Poland

Different country.

Same nightmare.

Over 100 people lived there —

all from different countries.

Each room had 8 to 10 men crammed inside.

In places like this, **strength decides everything**.

The **alpha male** becomes the boss.

One of those guys — from Armenia — was feared by everyone.

Later, I found out he had been training Muay Thai for years.

Some said he was a **champion**.

He was bigger than me.

Drank a lot.

Maybe used drugs too.

I didn't like him from day one.

Once, I told him:

— "Let's go outside. One-on-one."
He refused.

One night, I was walking to the bathroom.
Wearing just underwear —
normal for Russians and Belarusians.
A group of guys made a comment:
— "Hey, that's not okay."
I replied with something short and walked on.
Maybe that ticked him off.

Later, he stopped me:
— "Sit down. We need to talk."
I said:
— "I don't want to talk. Let's go outside."
He said:
— "If I get up... you'll go down."
I replied:
— "Let's see."

He got up.
Came at me.
There was a wall behind me.
No room to move.
I threw a fast combo to his face —
he charged in —
we tangled.
Somehow, I ended up on top.
But as I raised my hand to strike, his friends grabbed me.
— "Why are you doing this?" I asked.
— "We don't know you," they said.

They held me back while he charged again.
He tried to knee me in the face.
That would've knocked me out —
maybe worse.
But I moved just in time.
He elbowed me.
Landed it.
People pulled us apart.
We kept kicking at each other while being held.
He was screaming:
— "I'll kill you! I'll rape you! I'll bring my friends!"
It wasn't just talk.
They said he waited **all night** to fight me again.
I wrapped my hands every morning.
I was ready.
My wife begged me not to go to work.
But I did.
He never showed up.

Later, I saw him outside a store.
His eye was black and swollen shut.
He stared at me —
but said nothing.
Eventually, he **left the country**.
Some of his buddies came up to me:
— "Who did that to him?"
I said:
— "Me."
They didn't believe me.
I didn't look like a fighter.
Maybe that's why I always wanted to **become one**.

In the Eastern male world?
Short, skinny guys are only respected
after they punch someone in the face.

Final Advice

Don't let others walk over you.
If someone crosses the line —
and talking doesn't work —
stand your ground.
Yes, it's always better to avoid violence.
But in some environments?

Stupid people only understand stupid methods.

25

Final Chapter. The Law of Attraction

All the pain I went through —

the fights, the poverty, the addiction, the chaos —

I brought it all into my life myself.

Yes, you read that right.

Every single thing you've read in this book —

I believe **I attracted it into my reality.**

Now you might be thinking:

"What kind of nonsense is this guy talking about?"

Let me explain.

Around the age of thirty-three, I came across a powerful philosophy:

The Law of Attraction.

The idea is simple —

our thoughts, emotions, and beliefs directly shape our reality.

Whatever we constantly think about, visualize, and believe...

eventually becomes **real**.

If you fill your head with negativity — "I'm unlucky," "Nothing works out for me,"

"I'm just meant to suffer" —

then that becomes your life.

But if you **truly believe** that you're strong, healthy, and on the way to success —

that starts becoming real too.

Of course, just dreaming and waiting on the couch won't do it.

You still need to act.

You still need to hustle.

But the mindset behind your actions?

That changes everything.

To live a good life, you need:

- A clear vision.
- A direction.
- A daily dose of **gratitude**.

Start with being thankful for the basics:

- Your arms.
- Your legs.
- The fact that you're not in a hospital bed.
- The roof over your head.
- The food in your fridge.
- Your family.
- Your health.
- This very moment of peace.

If you can feel gratitude for the little things —
you open the door to much, much more.

Faith helps, too.
For most of my life, I didn't believe in anything.
I never prayed. I never went to church.
I thought it was all nonsense.
But since starting my current job — working in a Catholic school —
I've prayed almost every day.
And something has changed in me.
I find peace.
I find light.
I find hope.
Maybe it's faith.
Maybe it's energy.
Maybe it's simply the discipline of looking upward instead of downward.
But I know this much:
Something shifted.

One book that helped me a lot is called *The Way to a Happy Life.*
It touches on spiritual growth, positive energy —

and yes, the Law of Attraction.

I'm telling you:

This law is always working.

Every second.

Whether you believe in it or not.

So if you constantly dwell on anger, fear, and resentment —

don't be surprised when that's exactly what you get.

That's what my life looked like back then — my mind was completely consumed by dark, destructive thoughts.

This book isn't a spiritual manual, and I won't go deeper into the theory.

I just want to **point you in the right direction.**

Let me leave you with this truth:

I believe that every hardship in my life —

I somehow called it in.

And I believe that every blessing I now have —

I **created** it too.

Not by magic.

But by belief, action, consistency, and refusing to give up.

Sometimes, I feel like **something guides me** —

Like when I got into university.

Like when I met the right people at the right time.

Some people call it "luck."

I call it alignment.

There are hundreds of books, videos, and mentors out there talking about personal energy, abundance, and creating your own life.

Please — **read at least one of them**.

Watch *The Secret* on YouTube.

Laugh if you want — but it changed my life.

And it might just change yours too.

My final advice:

Believe.

Act.

Be grateful.

Focus only on what lifts you up —

not what pulls you down.

And over time —

little by little —

your life **will** change.

You'll be amazed how powerful you really are.

I wish you all the best, my friend.

From the bottom of my heart.

26

Life Advice Recap

My 14 Most Important Lessons from Life

I. Surroundings shape you.

Cut off toxic people. If you spend time with losers, you'll become one. Surround yourself with people who are better than you — and learn from them.

II. Do sports.

I understand that your society might be gentler. But still — for a man, a guy, or a boy, it's crucial to train. Taking care of your body means caring for your spirit.

III. Pursue what you love.

If you truly love something — go for it, no matter what. Passion is the key to success. Don't be afraid to talk about it. Don't be afraid to chase it.

IV. Family first.

Your family are the most important people in your life. They're the only ones who will truly support you when things fall apart.

V. Limit alcohol.

Alcohol destroys dreams, families, and self-respect. You don't need it to enjoy life.

VI. Be careful who you date.

Don't date girls who still want to party and "have fun." Choose wisely. Some relationships will only drain your energy and push you backwards.

VII. Believe in yourself.

Never think you can't do something. Just believe it — and take action. One small step at a time.

VIII. Learn the language. (for immigrants)

Learn the language of the country you move to! It gives you independence, confidence, and options.

IX. Chase your dream.

Even if you think it's too late — it's not. With enough effort, your dream will come true. Just don't give up too early.

X. Work hard — even in small jobs.

Whatever job you do — do it as well as you possibly can. People will notice and respect you.

XI. Accept success.

Believe in yourself. Accept praise for your hard work. Don't

downplay your wins. Own them.

XII. Try new things.

Don't be afraid to try something new — even if it sounds crazy. It might just change your life. The internet is full of opportunities.

XIII. Be strong when you have to.

Don't be afraid to use strength when it's really necessary. Don't let others think you're weak. Words don't always work — sometimes, fists speak louder.

XIV. Master your mind.

Watch "The Secret" on YouTube.

Learn how the Law of Attraction works — and how your thoughts shape your reality.

Be grateful. Be focused. Be kind.

✅ ***You have more power than you think.***

👣 ***Keep going. You're capable of creating a new life — one step at a time.***

Illustrations were created using artificial intelligence tools under the close supervision of the author, who personally reviewed, edited and approved each image.

27

Your Notes

Printed in Dunstable, United Kingdom

65123410R00090